BEAN

LIFE CYCLES

Words that look like **this** can be found in the glossary on page 24.

BookLife
PUBLISHING

©2021
BookLife Publishing Ltd.
King's Lynn
Norfolk PE30 4LS

All rights reserved.
Printed in Malaysia.

A catalogue record for this book is available from the British Library.

ISBN: 978-1-83927-156-4

Written by:
Kirsty Holmes

Edited by:
Shalini Vallepur

Designed by:
Danielle Webster-Jones

CONTENTS

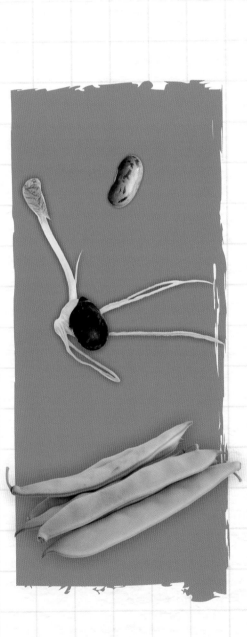

WHAT IS A LIFE CYCLE?

All animals, plants and humans go through different stages of their life as they grow and change. This is called a life cycle.

Human life cycle

Baby ➤ Child ➤ Adult

WHAT IS A BEAN?

A bean is a type of plant. A plant is a living thing that can make its own food from water and sunlight. The bean is the **edible** seed of the plant.

Oval-shaped and kidney-shaped seeds are called beans. Round seeds are peas.

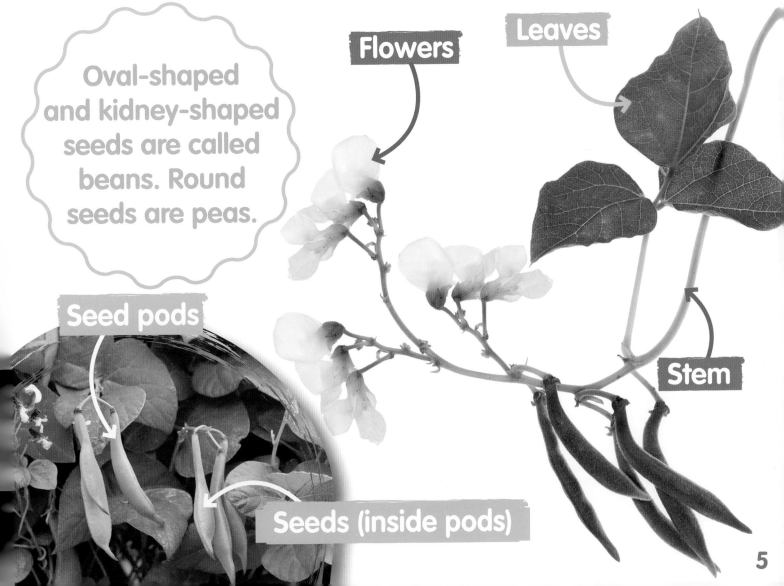

Flowers

Leaves

Seed pods

Stem

Seeds (inside pods)

SEEDS

The seeds grow inside a special case, called a seed pod. Each flower makes more than one seed. The seeds are kept safe inside the seed pod while they grow.

Runner bean

Seed pod

The bean is planted in soil. The soil is full of **nutrients** which the bean plant needs. The bean **absorbs** water in the soil. When the bean begins to grow, it splits open.

RADICLES

The bean will grow a small, special root called a radicle.
The radicle has been curled up inside the bean, ready to grow.
The radicle will grow down into the soil.

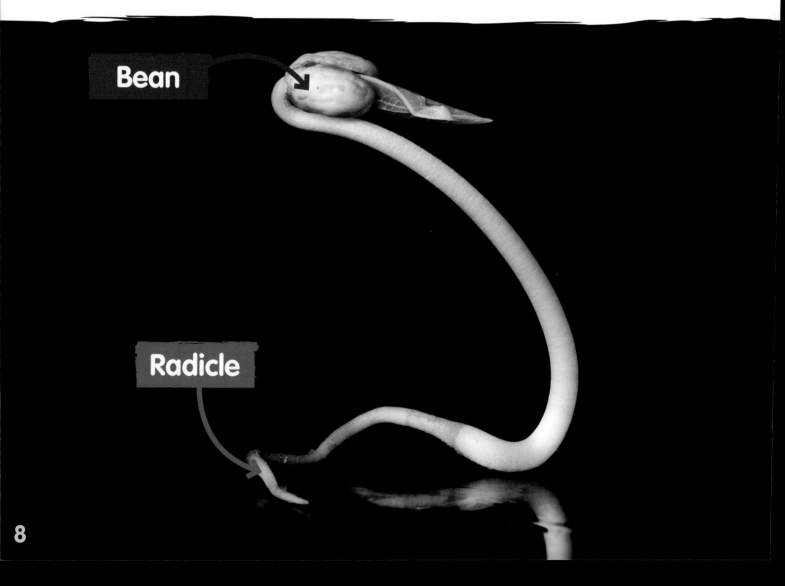

Bean

Radicle

Can you see the different radicles on these beans?

Roots start to grow from the radicle. The roots absorb water and nutrients from the soil. The radicle and roots help to **anchor** the plant into the soil.

SPROUTS

The bean will grow a short stem and a pair of small leaves. This tiny plant is called a shoot. Sometimes it is called a sprout.

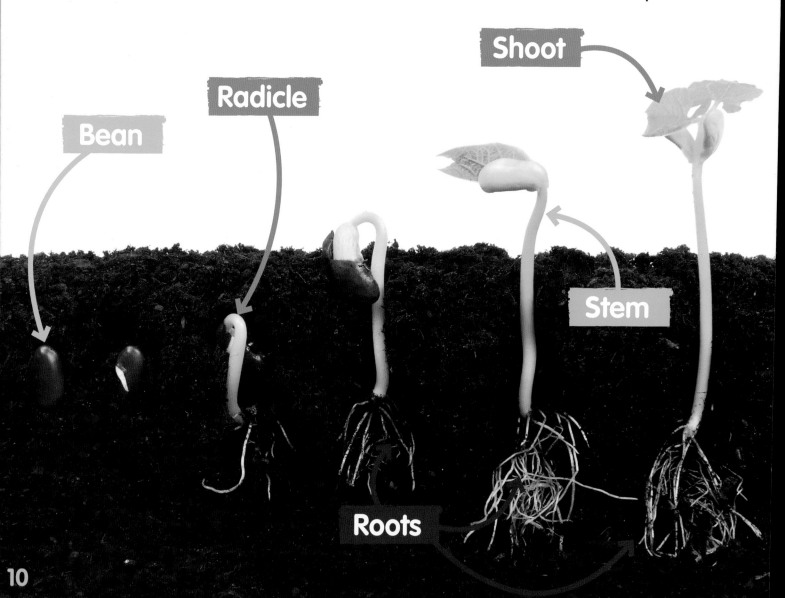

Shoot

Radicle

Bean

Stem

Roots

The shoot reaches out of the ground and up towards the light. The leaves take in sunlight. The plant uses the sunlight to make its food.

LEAVES

The tiny shoot will grow... and grow! The stem will become long, and new leaves will grow along it.

Many types of bean will grow very long and some like to climb up things.

Some beans also grow tendrils. These are long curly threads that grow from the plant and grab onto anything they can hang on to. They help to hold the plant up.

Tendril

Tendrils are curly and spiral-shaped to help them tangle and grip.

FLOWERS

After a few weeks, the plant will grow some flowers.
The flowers are small and come in lots of different colours.

These runner bean flowers are red.

The flowers are visited by bees and other creatures. These creatures are known as pollinators. They carry a special powder called pollen from flower to flower. This **fertilises** the plant.

BEANS

When the bean pod is picked and opened, there will be a row of beans inside it. The beans are ready to eat when they are plump and fat.

Beans are delicious and good for you. Make sure you ask a grown-up before you pick any.

If the pod is not picked, it will dry up and the beans will change colour. The dry pod will crack. Then the beans will fall to the soil, ready to begin the life cycle again.

Soybeans

TYPES OF BEAN

There are lots of different types of bean, and beans are eaten all over the world. Beans are full of **protein**. They can be dried and kept for a long time and are very delicious!

How many colours can you count?

Beans can be eaten while young. Sometimes the pod can be eaten too. The beans are **harvested**, then either cooked and eaten or dried.

WORLD RECORD BREAKERS

Longest Green Bean

The longest green bean in the world was grown by H Hurley from North Carolina in the US. The bean was grown in 1996 and was an amazing 121.9 centimetres long!

Chop Chop!

The record for the most baked beans eaten with chopsticks in one minute is held by Chisato Tanaka from Tokyo, Japan. She ate 72 beans!

LIFE CYCLE OF A BEAN

1 The bean takes in water and grows a radicle.

2 The bean grows a stem and leaves.

LIFE CYCLES

4 Bean pods grow, full of new seeds.

3 The flowers are pollinated by bees and other creatures.

GET EXPLORING!

Why not plant a bean of your own, and watch the different stages as it grows? What kinds of beans grow where you live?

GLOSSARY

absorbs   takes in or soaks up

anchor   to hold something firmly in place

edible   safe to be eaten

fertilises   causes a plant to be able to grow fruit or a new version of itself

harvested   to have picked fully grown crops

nutrients   natural things that plants and animals need in order to grow and stay healthy

protein   a natural thing that does important jobs in the body and is an important part of a human diet

INDEX

PHOTO CREDITS

All images are courtesy of Shutterstock.com, unless otherwise specified. With thanks to Getty Images, Thinkstock Photo and iStockphoto. Front cover & 1 – photogal. 2 – leonori. 3 – HHelene, Sarah Marchant, ConstantinosZ. 4 – Stuart Jenner, kdshutterman, szefei, Monika Bodova. 5 – Potapov Alexander, Jiri Vaclavek. 6 – Victoria Tucholka. 7 – Africa Studio. 8 – Alica Moser. 9 – images72. 10 – Bogdan Wankowicz. 11 – KPG_Payless. 12 – KIRAYONAK YULIYA. 13 – Tamara Kulikova. 14 – Richard Griffin. 15 – daily_creativity. 16 – dcwcreations, Nataliia K. 17 – Mikhailov Studio. 18 – Galayko Sergey. 19 – VVVproduct. 20 – Shany Muchnik ,MIKHAIL GRACHIKOV, mything.. 21 – Narcissa Less, Jabirki Art, hvostik.. 22 – Jean Faucett, ag1100, Pavel Holub, Victoria Tucholka. Jessica Ruscello. 23 – Rawpixel.com.